Topic 13

Counting Money

Teacher Resource Masters

- Center Activities
- Vocabulary Cards
- Interactive Math Story
- Lesson Masters
  - Daily Spiral Review
  - Problem of the Day
  - Quick Check
  - Reteaching
  - Practice
  - Enrichment
- Assessment

Organized the way you teach!

All masters for the topic are in the pouch!

Grade 1

ISBN-13: 978-0-328-28390-3
ISBN-10: 0-328-28390-8
9 780328 283903 90000

Scott Foresman-Addison Wesley

enVisionMATH™

Scott Foresman
is an imprint of

PEARSON

pearsonschool.com

Editorial Offices: Glenview, Illinois • Parsippany, New Jersey • New York, New York
Sales Offices: Boston, Massachusetts • Duluth, Georgia • Glenview, Illinois
Coppell, Texas • Sacramento, California • Mesa, Arizona

ISBN-13: 978-0-328-28390-3
ISBN-10: 0-328-28390-8

Notes

Start Get one [number cube]. Get 18 red squares.
Give one game board to each player.
Take turns.

Try Toss the [number cube]. Say the number.
Look at the game board.
If you see coins for that number of cents, cover the coins.
Repeat until one player wins.

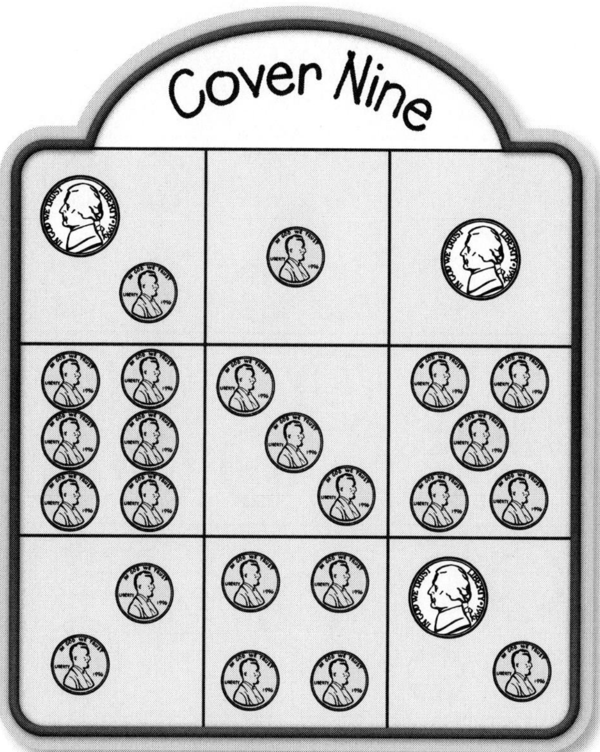

To win, be the first player to cover nine game spaces.

Play again!

Play a Game

Start Get dice. Get 18 red squares.
Give one game board to each player.
Take turns.

Try Toss the dice. Say the number in all.
Look on your game board.
If you see coins for that number of cents, cover the coins.
Repeat until one player wins.

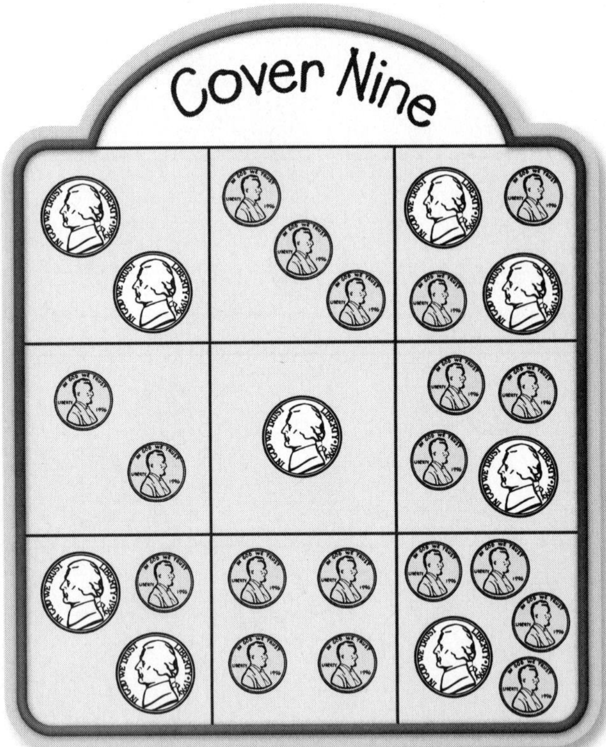

To win, be the first player to cover game spaces.

Try Again Play again!

Helping Hands

Put 1 2 3 4 5 6 in a bag.

Try Pick a tile. Put it in the square that has the same number.
Point to all the coins you need to buy that toy.
Take turns until the bag is empty.

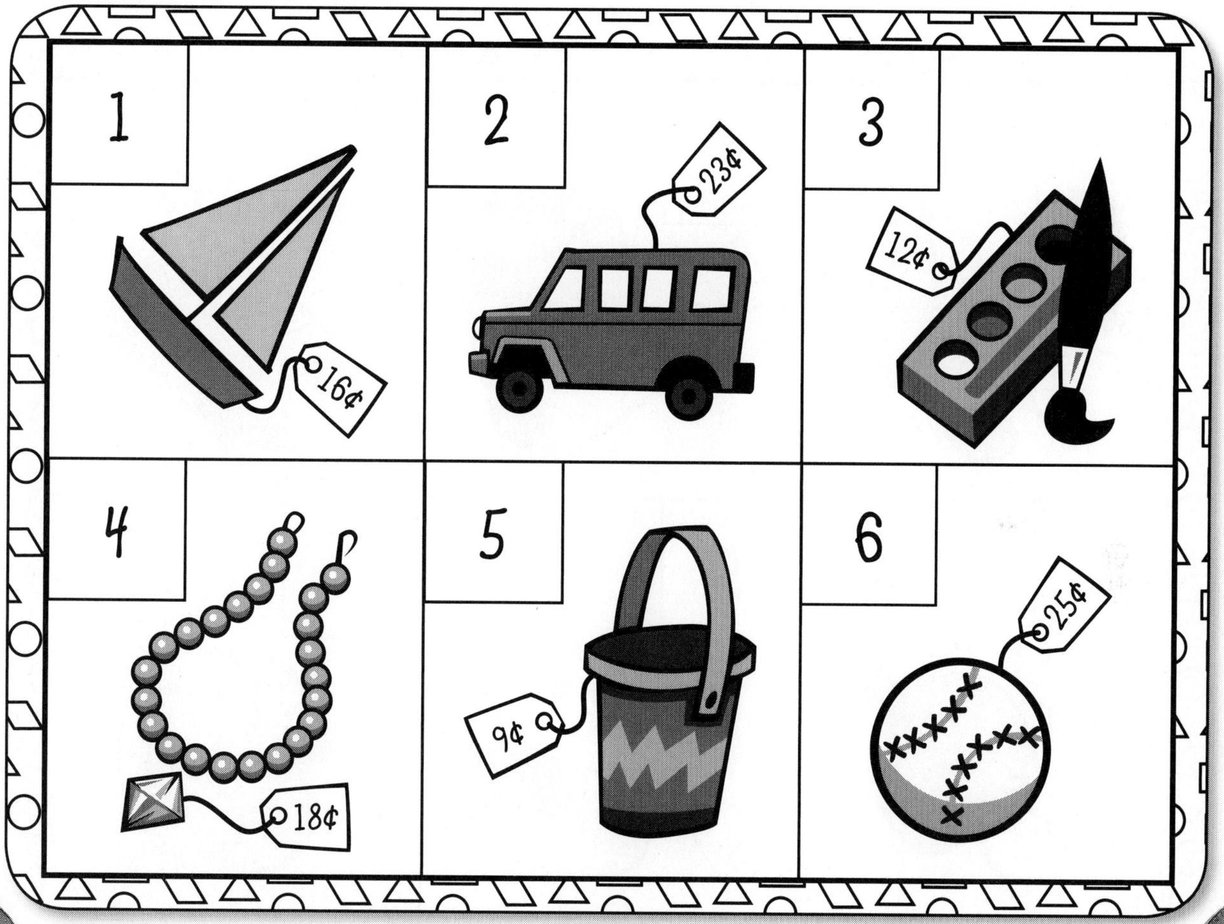

1 16¢	2 23¢	3 12¢
4 18¢	5 9¢	6 25¢

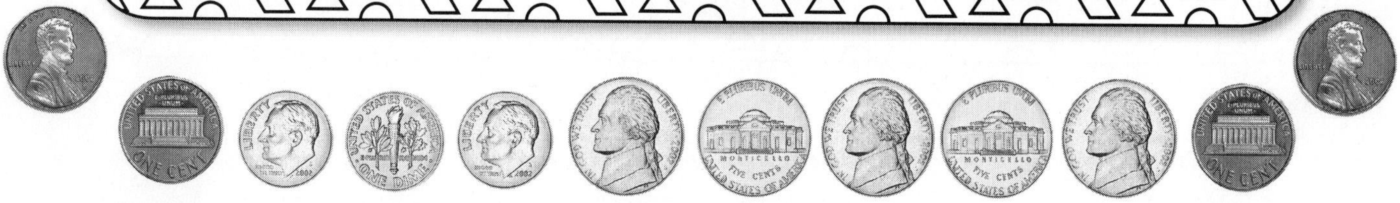

Try Again Put the tiles back in the bag. Repeat.
If there is more than one way to pay for a toy,
ask your partner to show another way.

Helping Hands

Put 1 2 3 4 5 6 in a bag.

Try Pick a tile. Put it in the square that has the same number.
Point to all the coins you need to buy that toy.
Ask your partner to show a different way to pay for that toy.
Take turns until the bag is empty.

1	2	3
30¢	25¢	27¢
4	5	6
13¢	17¢	23¢

Take turns. Point to all the coins you need to buy a toy.
Ask your partner to watch and name the toy you can buy.

Look and See

 Get one . Take turns.

 Toss the . Follow the directions. Make 25¢.

⚀	Use only nickels.
⚁	Use only pennies.
⚂	Use one dime and some other coins.
⚃	Use four nickels and some other coins.
⚄	Use one coin.
⚅	Use two dimes and some other coins.

Point to all the coins you need.

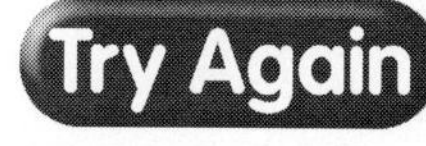 Repeat until each player gets 3 turns.

Look and See

Start Get one . Take turns.

 **Try** Toss the die. Follow the directions. Make 25¢.

Die	Directions
1	Use eight coins.
2	Use five coins.
3	Use nine coins.
4	Use three coins.
5	Use seven coins.
6	Use four coins.

Point to all the coins you need.

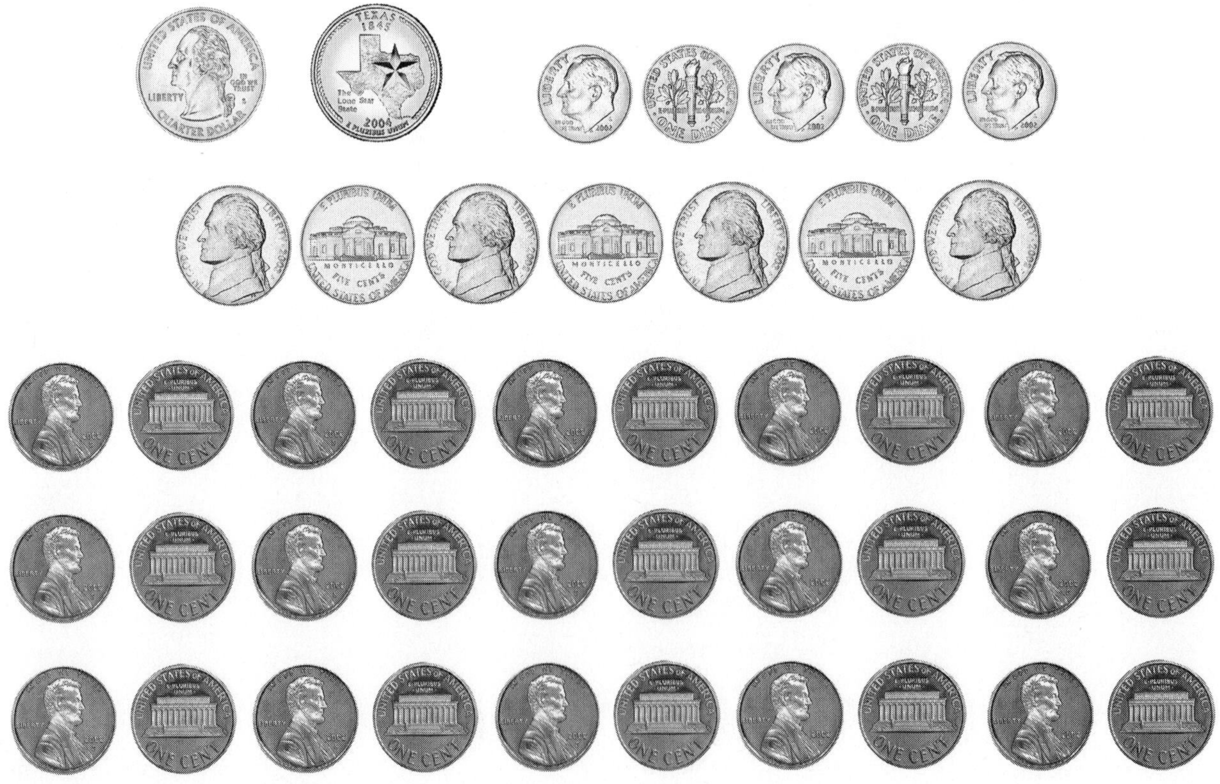

Try Again Repeat until each player gets 3 turns.

Play a Game

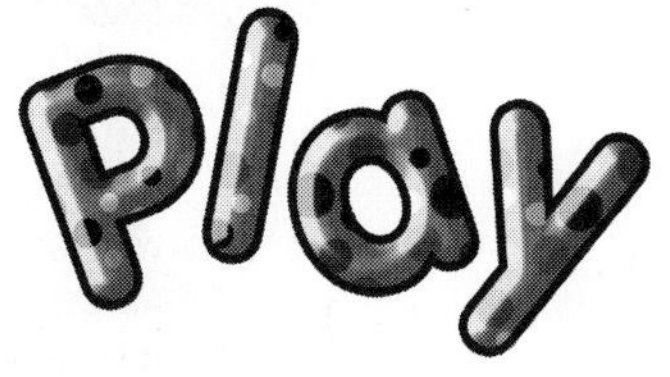

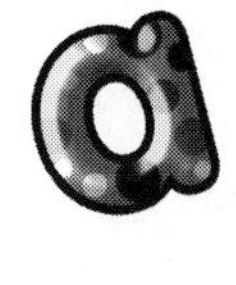

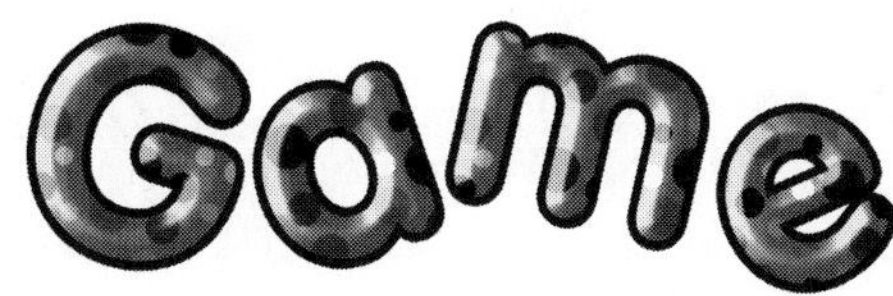

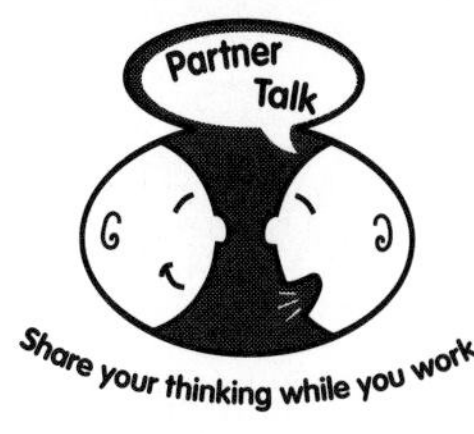

Start Get 12 red squares.
Cover each game space with a square.
Take turns.

Try Uncover two game spaces.

If one space names some coins, and the other space shows the value of those coins, keep the squares.

If not, put the squares back where they were.

Take turns until all the spaces are uncovered.

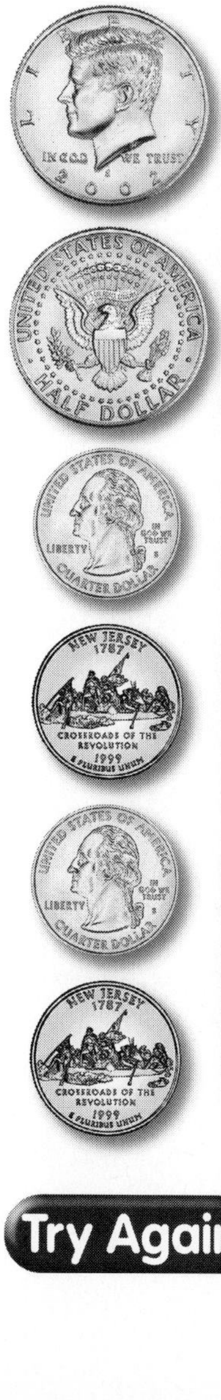

Memory Match

50¢	10 dimes	50¢	$1.00
2 half dollars	5 dimes	$1.00	2 quarters
$1.00	1 half dollar	4 quarters	50¢

To win, collect the most squares.

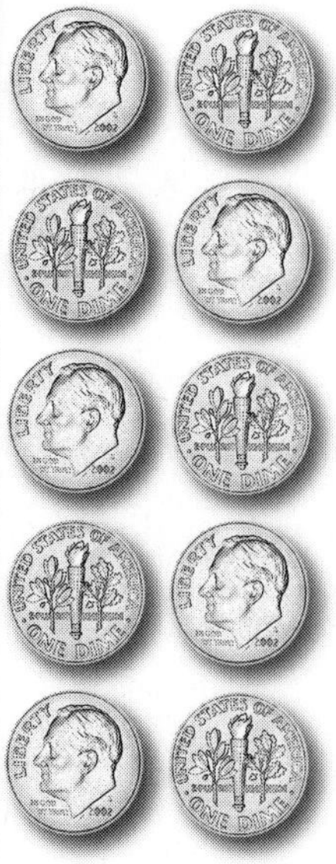

Try Again Play again!

Start Get 12 red squares.
Cover each game space with a square.
Take turns.

Try Uncover two game spaces.

If one space names some coins, and the other space shows the value of those coins, keep the squares.

If not, put the squares back where they were.

Take turns until all the spaces are uncovered.

1 half dollar 2 quarters	$1.00	50¢	10 nickels 5 dimes
1 quarter 2 dimes 1 nickel	50¢	2 quarters 5 dimes	3 dimes 4 nickels
$1.00	1 quarter 5 nickels	$1.00	50¢

To win, collect the most squares.

Try Again Play again!

Play a Game

Partner Talk
Share your thinking while you work.

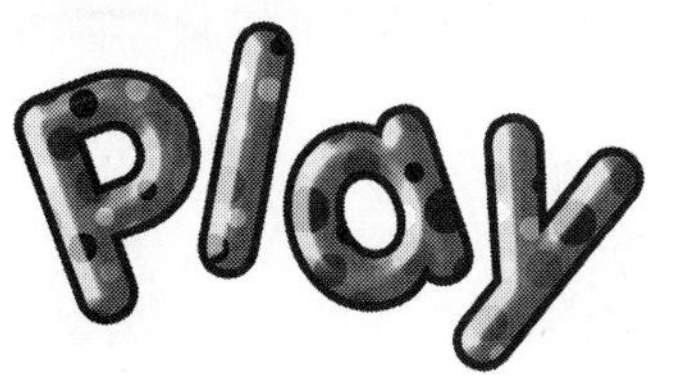

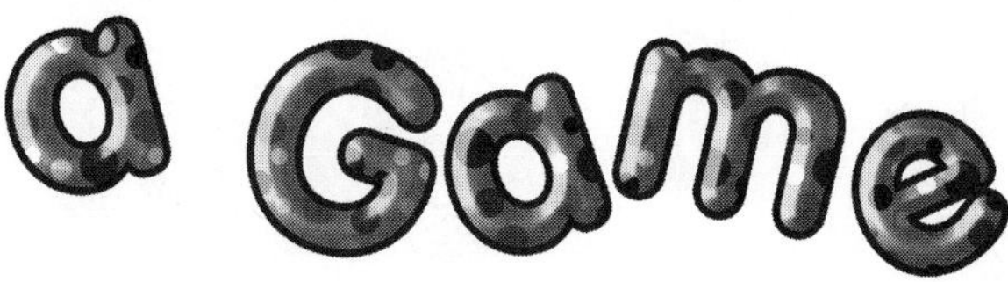

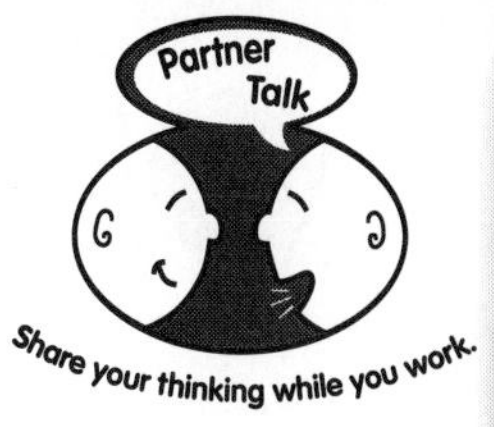

Start Get 12 red squares.
Cover each game space with a square. Take turns.

Try Uncover two game spaces.

If you find names of coins and the value of those coins, keep the squares.

If not, put the squares back where they were.

Take turns until all the spaces are uncovered.

Memory Match

three dimes	three nickels	two nickels	4¢
10¢	one dime and one penny	four pennies	11¢
8¢	15¢	30¢	one nickel and three pennies

To win, collect the most squares.

Try Again Play again!

Play a Game

Start Get 12 red squares.
Cover each game space with a square. Take turns.

Try Uncover two game spaces.

If the coins in one space have the same value as the coins in the other space, keep the squares.

If not, put the squares back where they were.

Take turns until all the spaces are uncovered.

Memory Match

one dime one nickel and one penny	two quarters	five nickels	one quarter one dime and one nickel
four dimes	one quarter	two dimes and ten pennies	four nickels
three nickels and one penny	three dimes	one dime and two nickels	five dimes

To win, collect the most squares.

Try Again Play again!

Look and See

Put 0 1 2 3 4 5 in a .

Get 10 red squares. Take turns until each player gets 5 turns.

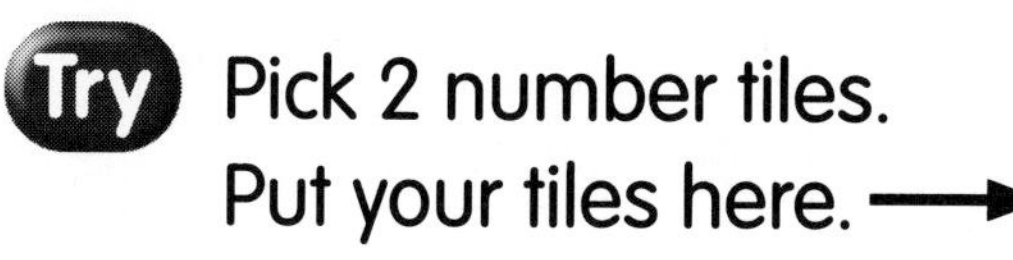

Try Pick 2 number tiles.
Put your tiles here. →

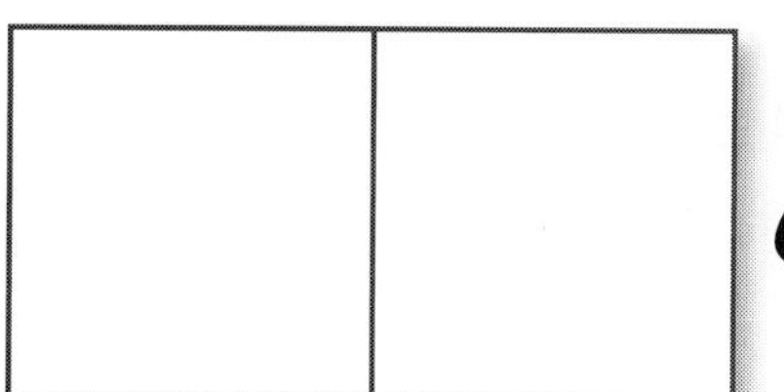

¢

Fruit	Price
Apple	23 ¢
Banana	10 ¢
Grapes	35 ¢
Cherries	17 ¢
Orange	26 ¢

Say the amount of money you have. Put a square next to a fruit if you have enough money to buy it. Tell your partner how many choices you have. Put the tiles back in the .

Fruit	Price
Lemon	12 ¢
Peach	29 ¢
Strawberries	48 ¢
Pear	14 ¢
Melon	25 ¢

Try Again This time, tell your partner which coins you can use to pay for the fruit you want to buy.

Look and See

Get 0 1 2 3 4 5 6 7 in a bag.

Get 10 red squares. Take turns until each player gets 5 turns.

Pick 2 number tiles.
Put your tiles here. →

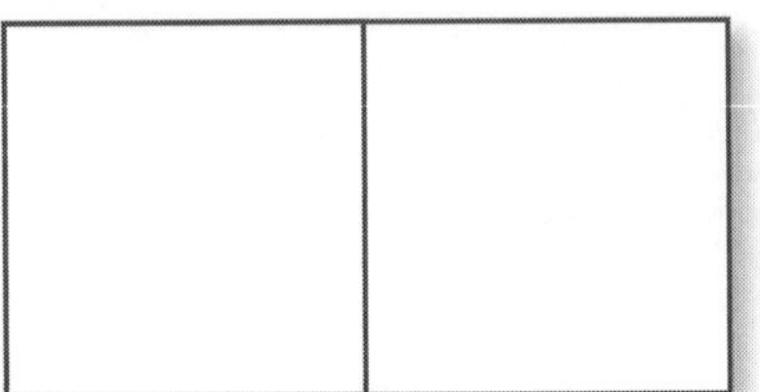

¢

Toys	Price
Doll	25 ¢
Boat	40 ¢
Ball	57 ¢
Top	28 ¢
Yo-yo	16 ¢

Say the amount of money you have. Put a square next to a toy if you have enough money to buy it. Tell your partner which toy that you can buy costs the most. Put the tiles back in the bag.

Toys	Price
Teddy Bear	36 ¢
Train	45 ¢
Truck	71 ¢
Car	39 ¢
Plane	61 ¢

Try Again This time, tell your partner which coins you can use to pay for the toy you want to buy.

Topic 13 ★
Center Activity Answers

13-1 Play a Game

Toss	Say	Cover
	1	1 penny
	2	2 pennies
	3	3 pennies
	4	4 pennies
	5	5 pennies, or 1 nickel
	6	6 pennies, or 1 nickel and 1 penny

13-2 Helping Hands

Pick 1 The toy sailboat costs 16¢.
Point to 1 dime, 1 nickel and 1 penny, or 3 nickels and 1 penny.

Pick 2 The bus costs 23¢.
Point to 2 dimes and 3 pennies, or 1 dime, 2 nickels, and 3 pennies, or 4 nickels and 3 pennies.

Pick 3 The paints cost 12¢.
Point to 1 dime and 2 pennies, or 2 nickels and 2 pennies.

Pick 4 The necklace costs 18¢.
Point to 1 dime, 1 nickel, and 3 pennies, or 3 nickels and 3 pennies.

Pick 5 The pail costs 9¢.
Point to 1 nickel and 4 pennies.

Pick 6 The ball costs 25¢.
Point to 2 dimes and 1 nickel, or 1 dime and 3 nickels, or 5 nickels.

13-3 Look and See

These answers are examples.

Toss	Point to
	5 nickels
	25 pennies
	1 dime and 3 nickels
	3 nickels and 1 dime
	1 quarter
	2 dimes and 1 nickel, or 2 dimes and 5 pennies

13-4 Play a Game

Memory Match

A	B	C	D
E	F	G	H
I	J	K	L

Spaces that Match

A and **F**, or **H**, or **J**
B and **D**, or **G**, or **I**
C and **F**, or **H**, or **J**
D and **B**, or **E**, or **K**
E and **D**, or **G**, or **I**
F and **A**, or **C**, or **L**
G and **B**, or **E**, or **K**
H and **A**, or **C**, or **L**
I and **B**, or **E**, or **K**
J and **A**, or **C**, or **L**
K and **D**, or **G**, or **I**
L and **F**, or **H**, or **J**

13-5 Play a Game

Memory Match

A	B	C	D
E	F	G	H
I	J	K	L

Spaces that Match

A and K　D and G
B and J　F and H
C and E　I and L

13-6 Look and See

These answers are examples.

Pick 1 0 ¢. **Cover** a banana.

Pick 1 2 ¢ or 1 3 ¢. **Cover** a banana or lemon.

Pick 2 3 ¢ or 2 4 ¢. **Cover** the banana, lemon, pear, cherries, or apple.

Pick 3 0 ¢ or 3 1 ¢ or 3 2 ¢ or 3 4 ¢. **Cover** the banana, lemon, pear, cherries, apple, melon, orange, or peach.

Pick 3 5 ¢ or 4 0 ¢ or 4 1 ¢ or 4 2 ¢ or 4 3 ¢ or 4 5 ¢. **Cover** any fruit except the strawberries.

Topic 13 ★★
Center Activity Answers

13–1 Play a Game

Toss	Say	Cover
	2	2 pennies
	3	3 pennies
	4	4 pennies
	5	5 pennies or 1 nickel
	6	1 penny and 1 nickel
	7	2 pennies and 1 nickel
	8	3 pennies and 1 nickel
	9	4 pennies and 1 nickel
	10	2 nickels
	11	1 penny and 2 nickels
	12	2 pennies and 2 nickels

13–2 Helping Hands

These answers are examples.

1 **Teddy bear 30¢** point to 3 dimes; your partner points to 2 dimes,2 nickels

2 **Crayons 25¢** point to 2 dimes, 1 nickel; your partner points to 1 dime, 3 nickels

3 **Car 27¢** point to 2 dimes, one nickel, 2 pennies; your partner points to 1 dime, 3 nickels, 2 pennies

13–3 Look and See

These answers are examples.

Toss	Point to
	1 dime, 2 nickels, and 5 pennies
	5 nickels
	4 nickels and 5 pennies
	2 dimes and 1 nickel
	2 dimes and 5 pennies
	1 dime and 3 nickels

13–4 Play a Game

Memory Match

A	B	C	D
E	F	G	H
I	J	K	L

Spaces that Match

A and **B**, or **I**, or **K**
B and **A**, or **D**, or **G**
C and **E**, or **H**, or **J**
D and **B**, or **I**, or **K**
E and **C**, or **F**, or **L**
F and **E**, or **H**, or **J**
G and **B**, or **I**, or **K**
H and **C**, or **F**, or **L**
I and **A**, or **D**, or **G**
J and **C**, or **F**, or **L**
K and **A**, or **D**, or **G**
L and **E**, or **H**, or **J**

13–5 Play a Game

Memory Match

A	B	C	D
E	F	G	H
I	J	K	L

Spaces that Match

A and **I**   **D** and **E**
B and **L**   **G** and **J**
C and **F**   **H** and **K**

13–6 Look and See

These answers are examples.

Pick	Buy
* 10¢, 12¢, 13¢, 14¢, 15¢	No toy
* 16¢, 17¢, 20¢, 21¢, 22¢, 23¢, 24¢	Yo-yo
* 25¢, 26¢, 27¢	Doll or yo-yo

Name____

value Lesson 13–1	**penny** Lesson 13–1
nickel Lesson 13–1	**cent** Lesson 13–1

Instead of making 2-sided copies of this Words page and the Definitions page, you can copy the Definitions page, cut out the cards, and have students write the words on the other side of the cards.

Name________________________________

penny

A **penny** is worth
one cent or 1¢.

value

The **value** of one
penny is 1 cent.

cent

A penny is
1 **cent** (¢).

nickel

A **nickel** is worth
5 cents or 5¢.

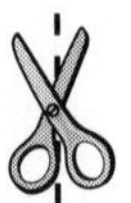

Name________________________________

dime

Lesson 13–2

quarter

Lesson 13–3

half dollar

Lesson 13–4

Instead of making 2-sided copies of this Words page and the Definitions page, you can copy the Definitions page, cut out the cards, and have students write the words on the other side of the cards.

Name________________________________

quarter

25 cents or 25¢

dime

10 cents or 10¢

half dollar

50 cents or 50¢

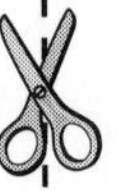

Name________________________________

dollar

Lesson 13–4

Instead of making 2-sided copies of this Words page and the Definitions page, you can copy the Definitions page, cut out the cards, and have students write the words on the other side of the cards.

dollar

$1.00 or 100¢

Oh, I must use a dime.

My friends can help.

Can you give me a dime?

______ nickels is the same as

______ dime.

fold down

This book belongs to:

____

Topic 13 Story

I Need A Coin

Written by Raven Jefferson Illustrated by Ken Gamage

I can get this!

I know I have enough.

I have 5 pennies.

5 pennies is ______ ¢

Oh, I must use a nickel.
My friends can help.
Can you give me a nickel?
_____ pennies is the same as
_____ nickel.

fold up

I can get this!
I know I have enough.
I have 2 nickels.
2 nickels is _____ ¢.

Name________________________________

1. Which tells about the model?

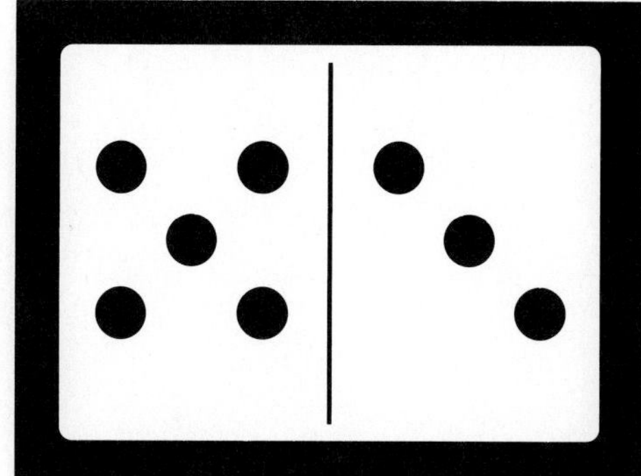

Ⓐ $5 - 3 = 2$

Ⓑ $3 + 0 = 3$

Ⓒ $5 + 0 = 5$

Ⓓ $5 + 3 = 8$

2. Rachel took 6 photos.
Kyle took 5 photos.
How many photos did they take altogether?

_____ photos

3. Circle the part that repeats.
Then extend the pattern

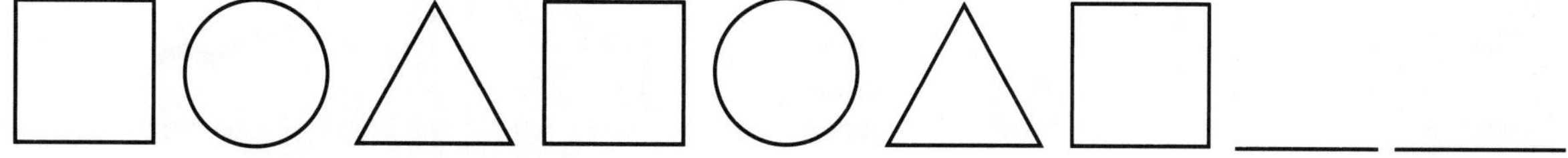

Problem of the Day 13-1

Skip count by ________.

There are ________

bananas altogether.

Read Aloud Look for a pattern. How many bananas in all?

Name ______________________________

1. Which is the value of the coins?

Ⓐ 7¢

Ⓑ 10¢

Ⓒ 11¢

Ⓓ 15¢

2. The cost of 2 apples is 10¢.
How much does 1 apple cost?

Ⓐ 10¢

Ⓑ 8¢

Ⓒ 6¢

Ⓓ 5¢

3. Draw a picture to solve.
Write the numbers.

How many nickels and pennies do you need to buy the bracelet?

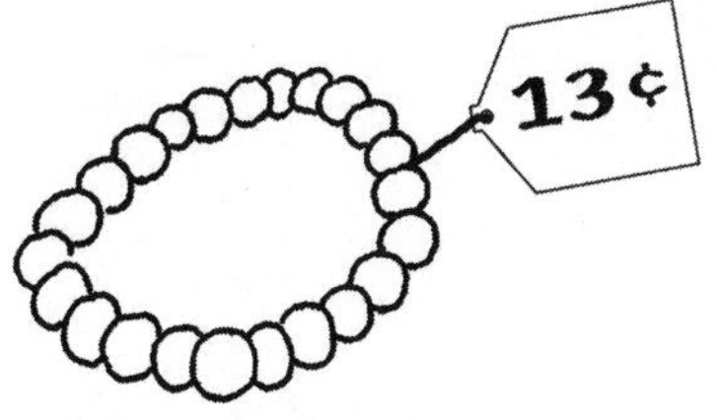

____________ nickels

____________ pennies

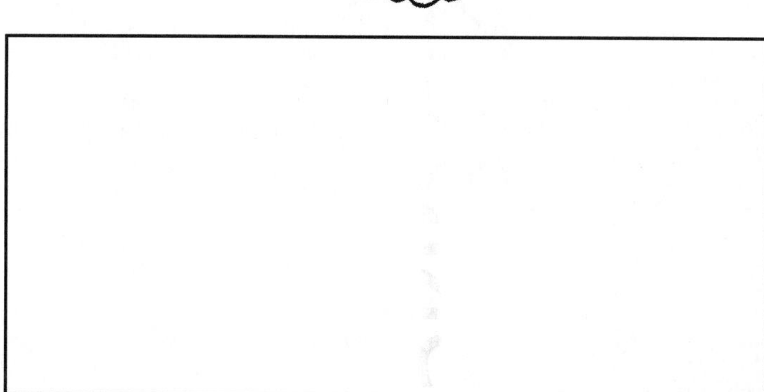

Name____________________

Values of Penny and Nickel

A nickel = 5 cents.
Skip count by 5s for nickels.

A penny = 1 cent.
Count by 1s for pennies.

Skip count by 5s for the nickels.
Then count on by 1s for the pennies.

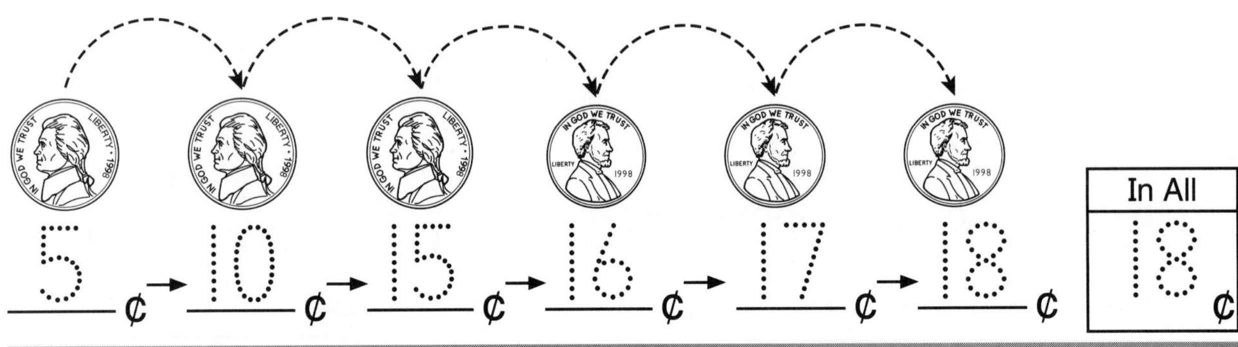

5 ¢ → 10 ¢ → 15 ¢ → 16 ¢ → 17 ¢ → 18 ¢

In All
18 ¢

Skip count by 5s and count on by 1s to find how much money in all.

1.

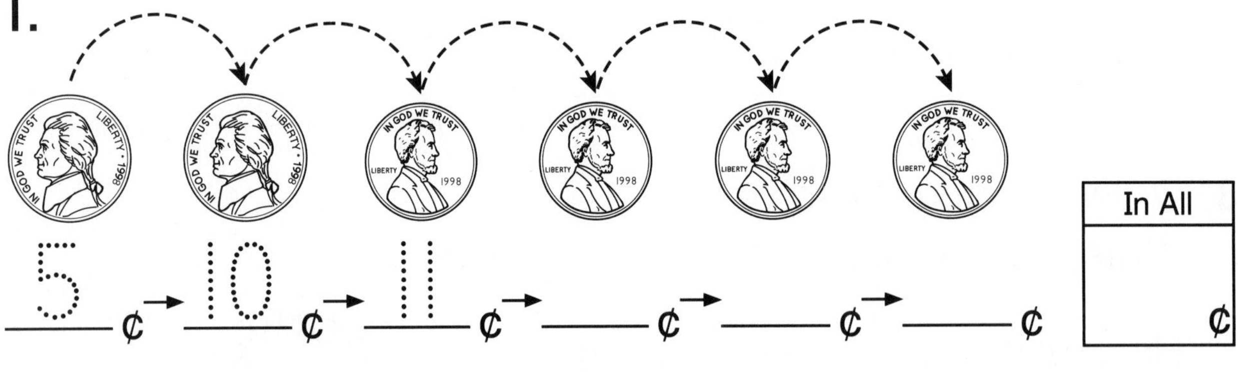

5 ¢ → 10 ¢ → 11 ¢ → ___ ¢ → ___ ¢ → ___ ¢

In All
¢

2.

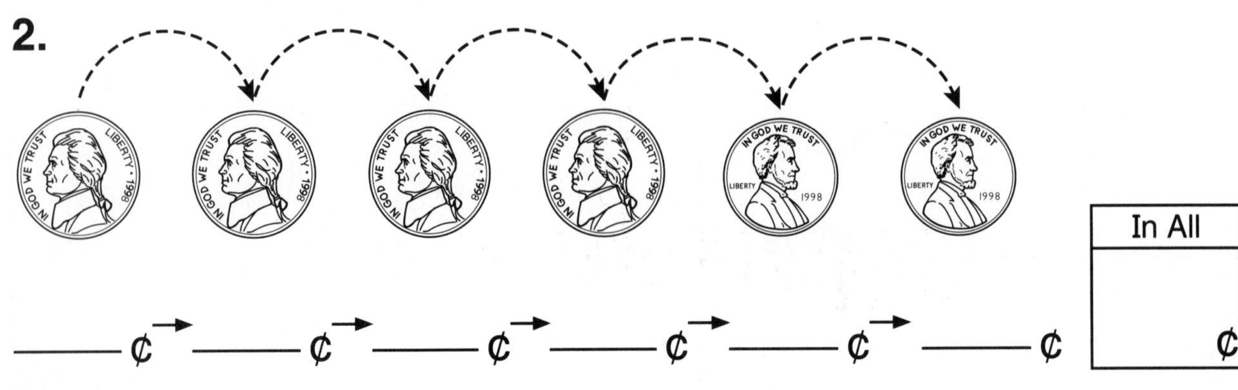

___ ¢ → ___ ¢ → ___ ¢ → ___ ¢ → ___ ¢ → ___ ¢

In All
¢

Name____________________

Values of Penny and Nickel

1. Count on. Then write how much money in all.

5¢ 6¢ 7¢ 8¢ 9¢

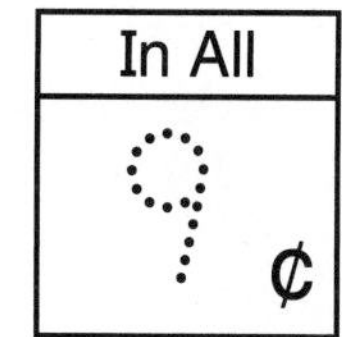

In All
9 ¢

2.

____¢ ____¢ ____¢ ____¢ ____¢

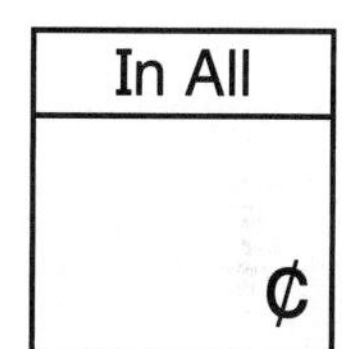

In All
¢

Circle the coins that match each price.

3.

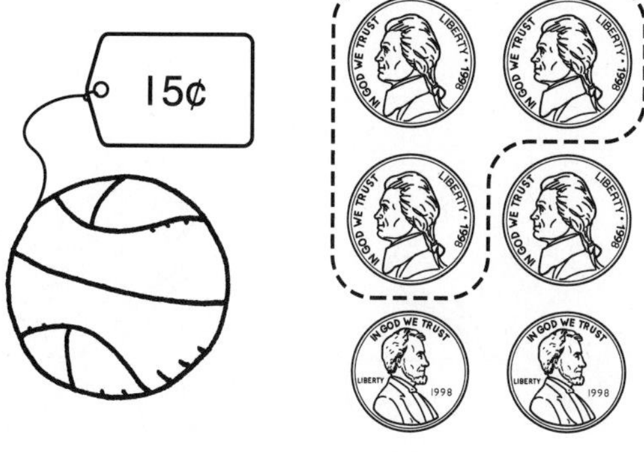

4.

Reasoning

5. Jan has 6 coins.
She has 2 nickels.
The rest are pennies.
How much money does Jan have?

15¢  Ⓐ

14¢  Ⓑ

13¢  Ⓒ

12¢  Ⓓ

Name______________________________

Shopping for Toys

Number Sense

Count the money in each pocket.
Write how much money in all.
Then circle the toy you can buy.

1.

______¢ in all

2.

______¢ in all

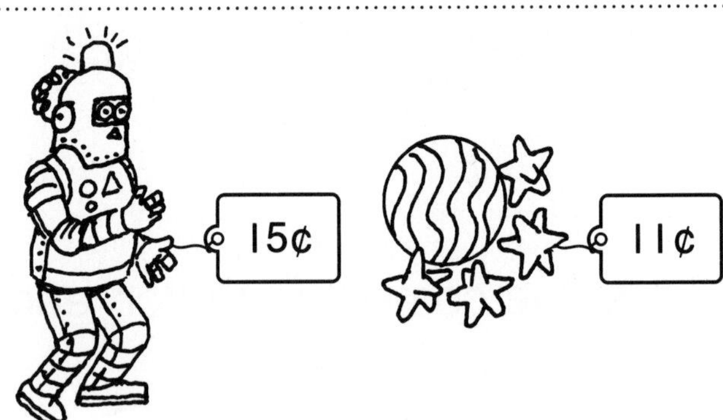

3.

______¢ in all

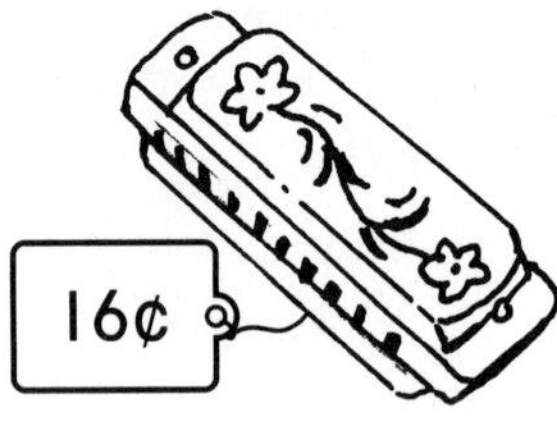

4.

______¢ in all

Name____

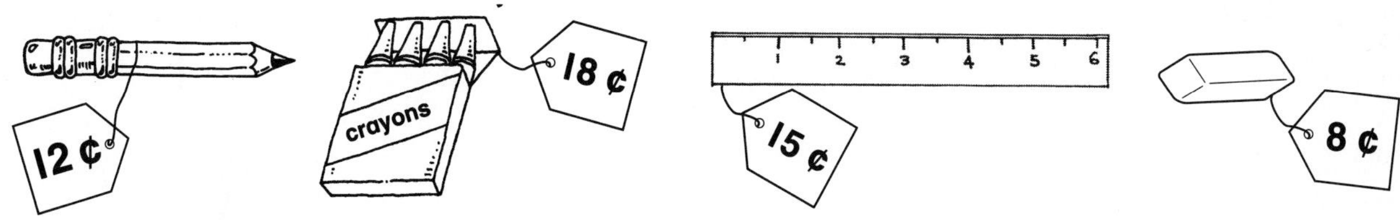

1. Mia wants to buy a box of crayons. Which coins should she use?

Ⓐ 

Ⓑ 

Ⓒ 

Ⓓ 

2. How much money does Carlos need to buy the pencil and the eraser?

Ⓐ 12¢

Ⓑ 20¢

Ⓒ 27¢

Ⓓ 30¢

3. Rico has 2 nickels and 3 pennies.
Gina has 12 pennies.
Who has more money?

____

Problem of the Day 13-2

Solve.
Mia spent 10¢.
What did
she buy?

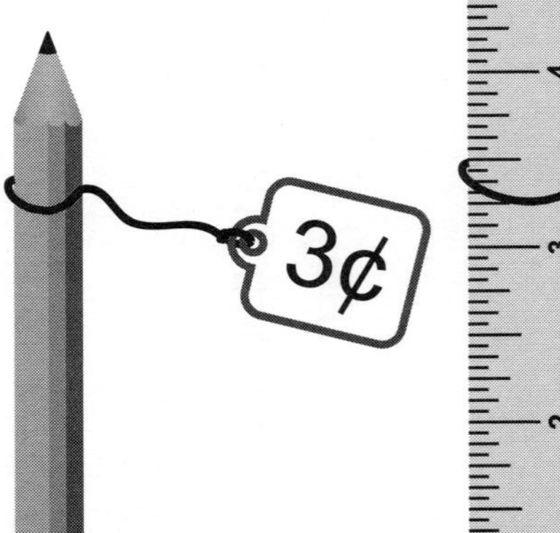

Problem of the Day 13-2

Name____

1. Cecelia has 25¢.
Which is the missing coin?

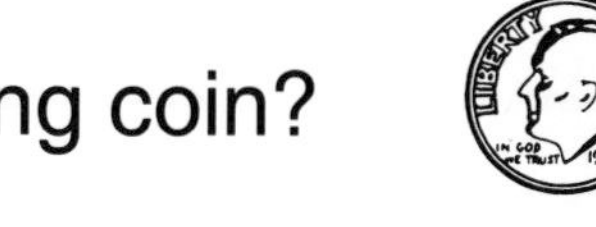

Ⓐ penny

Ⓑ nickel

Ⓒ dime

Ⓓ quarter

2. Dan has 35¢.
Which coins does he have?

Ⓐ  D D D N N

Ⓑ D D D N

Ⓒ D D N N

Ⓓ D N N N

3. Draw a picture to solve.
Write the numbers.

Lupe has 16¢ in her bank.
How many dimes, nickels, and pennies could she have?

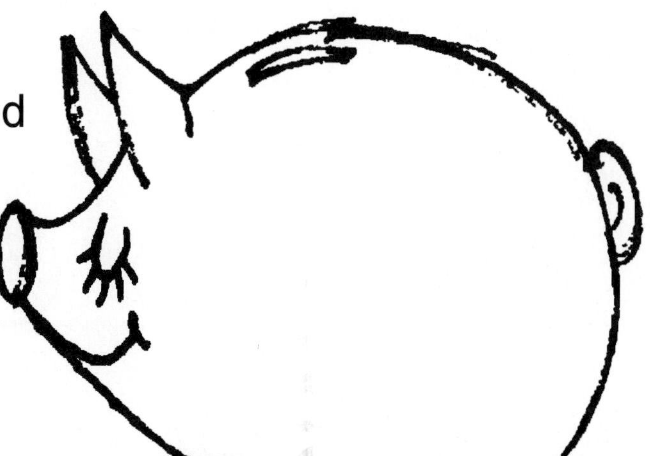

________ dimes

________ nickels

________ pennies

Name____________________________

Values of Penny, Nickel, and Dime

A dime = 10 cents.
Skip count by 10s for dimes.

A penny = 1 cent.
Count by 1s for pennies.

Skip count by 10s. Then count on by 1s.

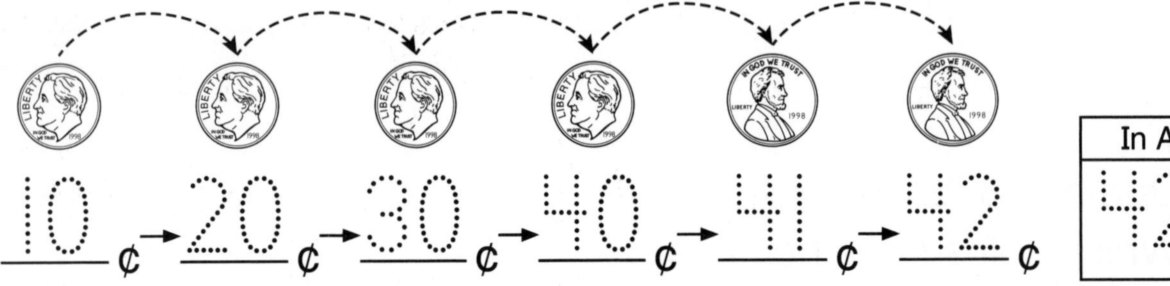

10 ¢ → 20 ¢ → 30 ¢ → 40 ¢ → 41 ¢ → 42 ¢

In All
42 ¢

Skip count by 10s and count on by 1s to find how much money in all.

1.

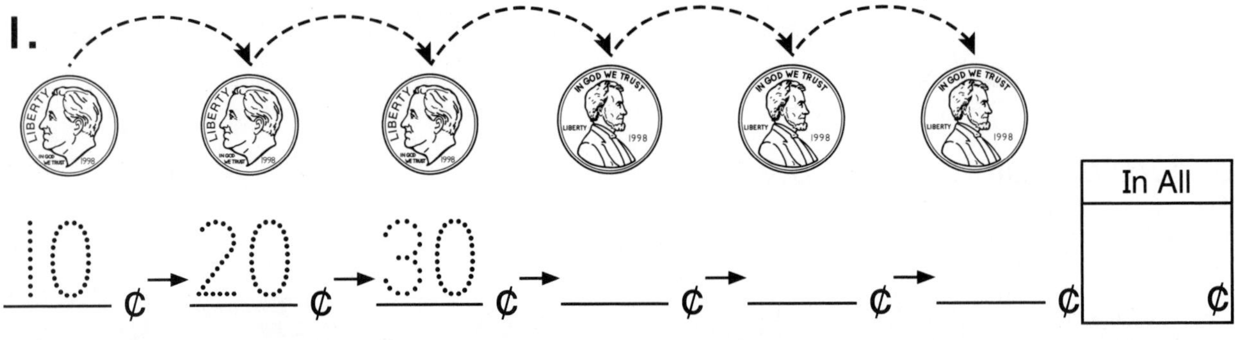

10 ¢ → 20 ¢ → 30 ¢ → ____ ¢ → ____ ¢ → ____ ¢

In All
¢

2.

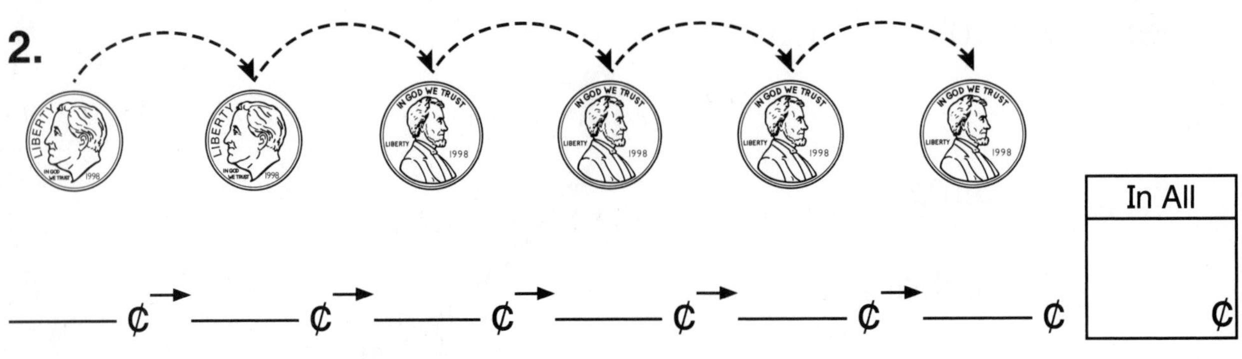

____ ¢ → ____ ¢ → ____ ¢ → ____ ¢ → ____ ¢ → ____ ¢

In All
¢

Name____

Values of Penny, Nickel, and Dime

Circle the coins you could use to buy each item.

1. 

2. 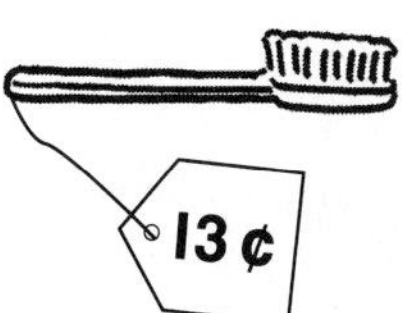

3. 

Journal

4. An apple costs 7¢. An orange costs 8¢. A banana costs 9¢. You have 2 dimes. Which 2 pieces of fruit could you buy?

   ____________ and ____________

   How much money would you have left?

   ______¢

Name______________________________

School Supplies

Visual Thinking

Look at the 2 items.
Circle the item you want.
Then circle the coins to match the price.

1.

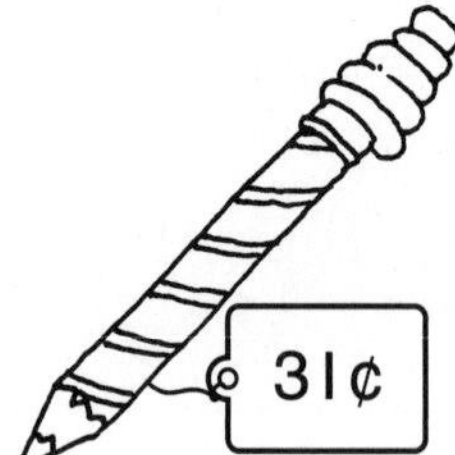

2.

3.

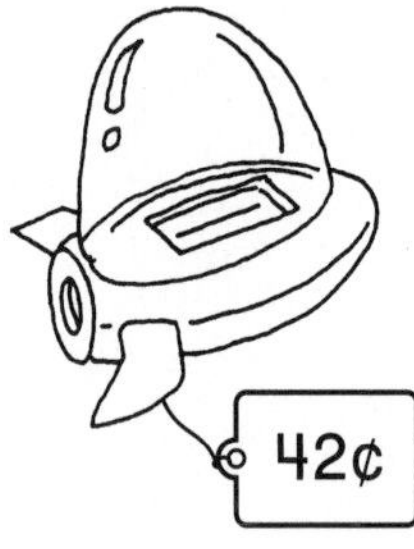

4.

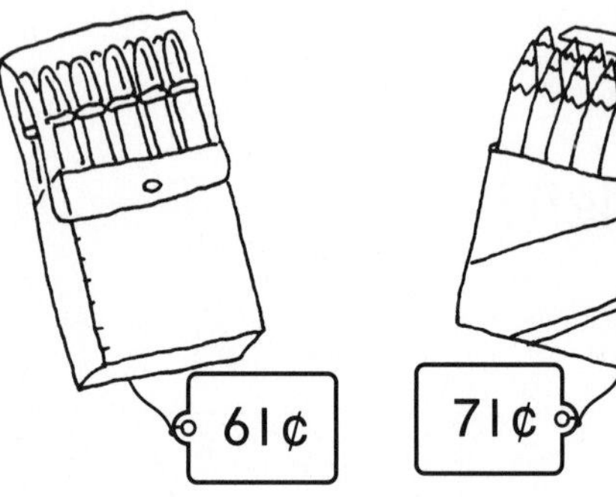

Name

1. Which coins can Denzel use to buy a glass of lemonade?

Ⓐ  

Ⓑ  

Ⓒ  

Ⓓ       

2. Meg has 1 dime and 4 nickels. How many glasses of lemonade can Meg buy?

Ⓐ 2

Ⓑ 3

Ⓒ 4

Ⓓ 6

3. Which shows parts of 10?

9 and 2	7 and 6	5 and 4	2 and 8
Ⓐ	Ⓑ	Ⓒ	Ⓓ

Problem of the Day 13-3

Mark has 8 coins. He has 2 dimes. The rest of his coins are nickels. How many nickels does Mark have?

Problem of the Day 13-3

Name ______________________________

1. Which tells the value of the coins?

Ⓐ 38¢

Ⓑ 33¢

Ⓒ 28¢

Ⓓ 18¢

2. Rosario has 40¢ in her pocket. Which coins does she have?

Ⓐ D D D N P P P

Ⓑ Q N N N

Ⓒ Q D D

Ⓓ N N N N N N N D

3. Draw a picture to solve. Write the numbers.

A magic kit costs 65¢. What is the fewest number of coins you can use to buy the magic kit?

________ quarters

________ dimes

________ nickels

Name________________________________

Value of Quarter

There are different ways you can make 25¢.

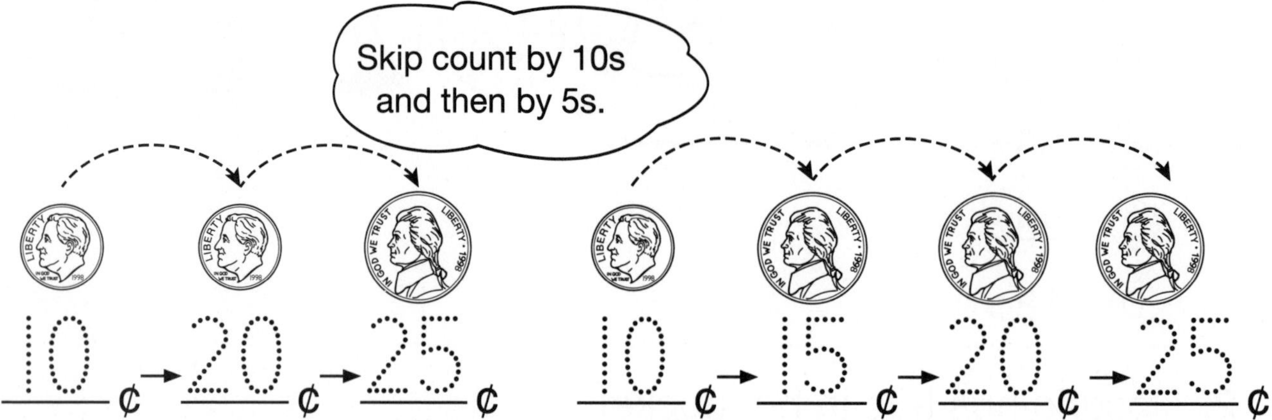

Count each group of coins.
Circle the group of coins in each row that equals 25¢.

1.

2.

3.

Visual Thinking

4. Chris has 4 coins in her purse.
They are worth 25¢ in all.
Draw the other 2 coins.

Name______________________________

Value of Quarter

Circle the coins that equal 25¢.

1. 

2. 

3. 

4. 

5. 

Number Sense

6. Kate has 25¢ in her purse.
Which coins does she have?

Name____________________________

Enrichment
13-3

Quarter Challenge

Patterns

Can you show 25¢ in 8 different ways?
Circle the way that shows the fewest coins.

	Dimes	Nickels	Pennies
1. 25¢	1	3	
2. 25¢			
3. 25¢			
4. 25¢			
5. 25¢			
6. 25¢			
7. 25¢			
8. 25¢			

Name________________________________

1. Gretchen uses these coins to buy a postcard.
How much does the postcard cost?

Ⓐ 22¢

Ⓑ 27¢

Ⓒ 37¢

Ⓓ 42¢

2. There are 7 tents.
Each tent holds 10 children.
How many campers
can the tents hold altogether?

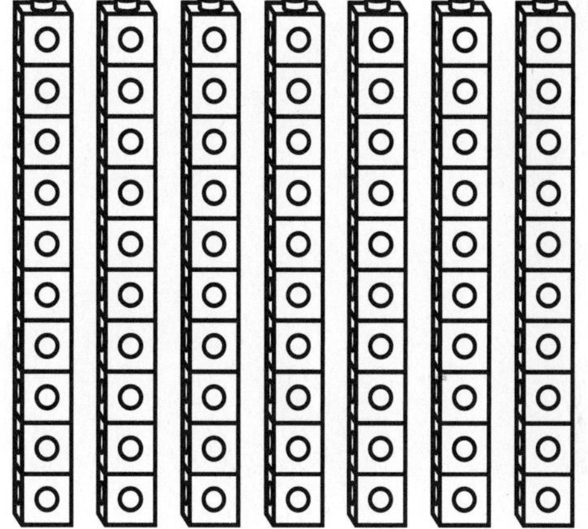

Ⓐ 77

Ⓑ 70

Ⓒ 17

Ⓓ 7

3. Giovanni found 25¢ under the couch.
Circle Giovanni's coins.

Problem of the Day 13-4

Read Aloud The pictures of presidents are found on many U.S. coins. A picture of Abraham Lincoln is on the penny and a picture of George Washington is on the quarter. What is the value of 2 "George Washington" coins and 3 "Abraham Lincoln" coins?

Problem of the Day
13-4

Name________________________________

1. Sandy wants to buy a newspaper for 50¢. Which coin does she need to have 50¢ altogether?

 Ⓐ  Ⓑ Ⓒ Ⓓ

2. John uses quarters to buy a juice box. The juice box costs $1.00. How many quarters does John use?

Ⓐ 1 quarter

Ⓑ 2 quarters

Ⓒ 3 quarters

Ⓓ 4 quarters

3. Circle coins to make $1.00. Draw boxes around different coins to show another way to make $1.00.

Name________________________________

Values of Half Dollar and Dollar

Here are some ways to show one dollar.

dollar bill

$1.00 = 100¢

dollar coin

 or 

$1.00 = 100¢

2 half-dollar coins

half-dollar = 50¢

2 half-dollars = 100¢

4 quarters

25¢ → 50¢ → 75¢ → 100¢

4 quarters = 100¢

Circle the group of coins in each row that makes $1.00.

1.

2.

3.

Name________________________________

Values of Half Dollar and Dollar

Circle the coins that equal $1.00.

1.        

2.      

3.       

Reasoning

4. Which shows the same amount?

Name________________________

Share and Share Alike

Each child should get 1 dollar. Circle the coins to show 1 dollar. Draw a line to each child.

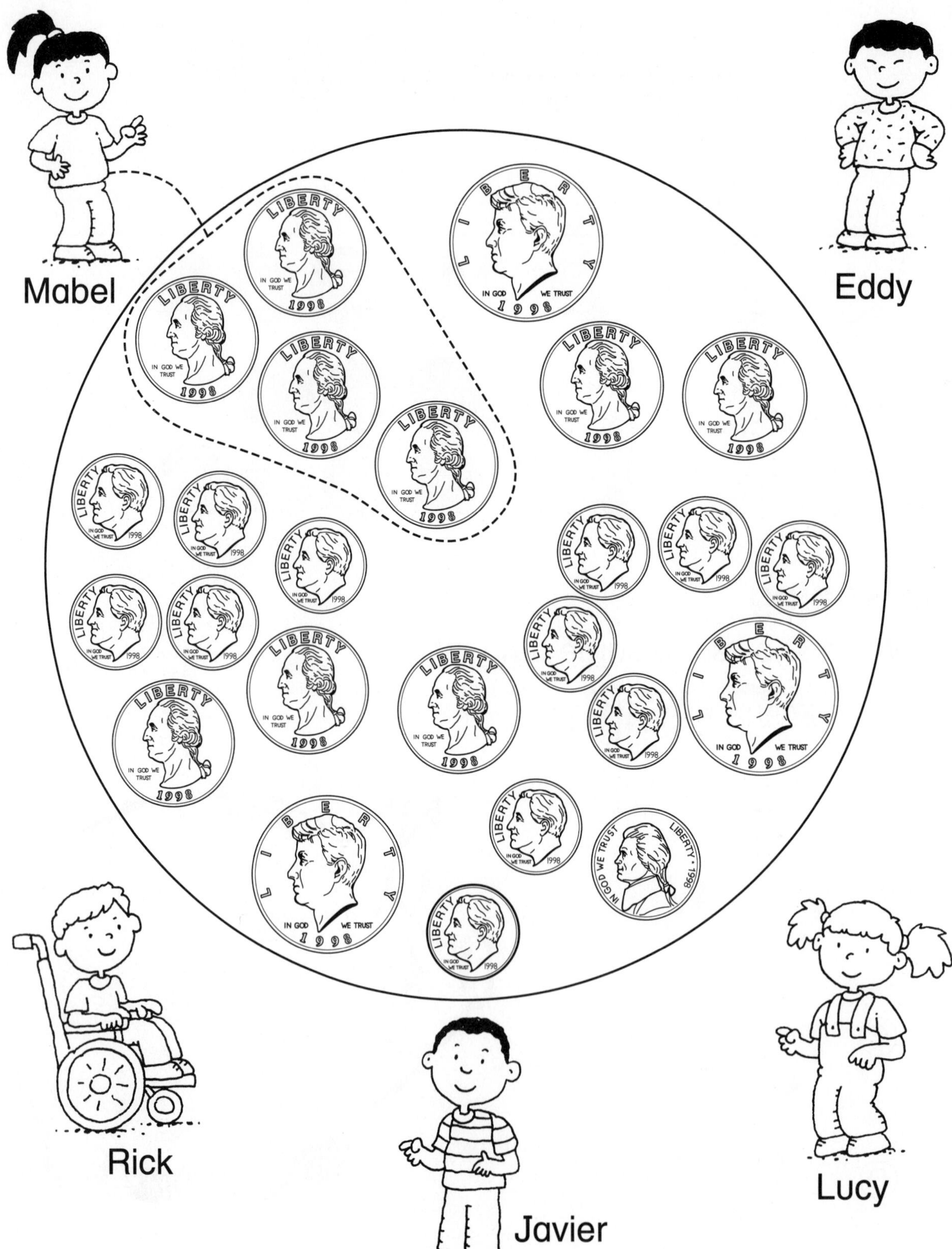

Name________________________________

1. Which solid figure is the same shape as the fish tank?

Ⓐ 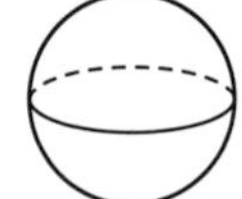

Ⓑ 

Ⓒ 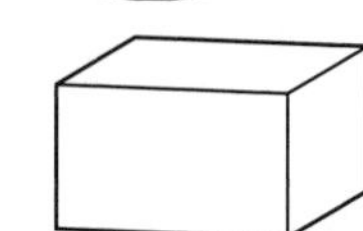

Ⓓ 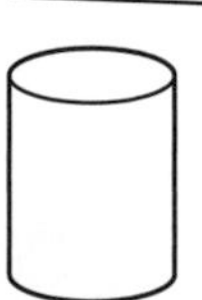

2. Kim has 5 dimes.
Which shows the same amount?

Ⓐ        

Ⓑ     

Ⓒ    

Ⓓ 

3. Write the missing numbers.

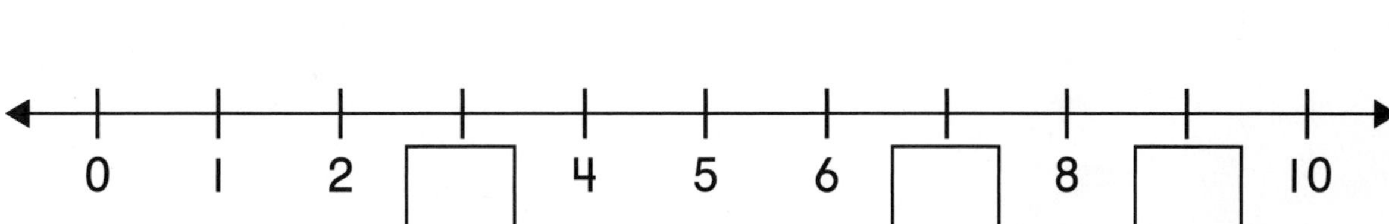

Problem of the Day 13-5

Matt has 50¢ in his bank.

Read Aloud Make an organized list. Show 4 different ways Matt can have 50¢.

Problem of the Day 13-5

Name ________________________________

Quick Check
13-5

1. Which shows how much money in all?

Ⓐ 25¢, 35¢, 45¢, 50¢, 55¢, 60¢

Ⓑ 40¢, 60¢, 65¢, 70¢, 75¢, 76¢

Ⓒ 50¢, 60¢, 70¢, 75¢, 80¢, 85¢

Ⓓ 50¢, 60¢, 70¢, 71¢, 72¢, 73¢

2. Eugene has 60¢.
He has 1 half dollar.
Which other coins does Eugene have?

Ⓐ quarter, dime

Ⓑ dime, dime

Ⓒ dime, nickel

Ⓓ nickel, nickel

3. Draw a picture to solve.
Then make a list.
What are two ways to
show 56¢?

Coins	H	Q	D	N	P
Way 1					
Way 2					

Way 1
Way 2

Name________________________

Counting Sets of Coins

Remember > stands for greater than.

Count the coins.
Start with the coin that is worth the most money.

50¢ 75¢ 85¢ 90¢ 91¢

In All
91 ¢

Skip count. Then write how much money in all.

1.

_____¢ _____¢ _____¢ _____¢ _____¢

In All
¢

2.

_____¢ _____¢ _____¢ _____¢ _____¢

In All
¢

Name______________________________

Practice
13-5

Counting Sets of Coins

Skip count. Then write how much money in all.

1.

_____¢ _____¢ _____¢ _____¢ _____¢

In All
¢

2.

_____¢ _____¢ _____¢

In All
¢

Journal

3. You have 50¢ in all.
What can you buy for lunch?
Be sure to include fruit.
How much will it cost?
How much will you have left?

____

____

Menu

Soup............19¢
Ham Sandwich...25¢
Apple............15¢
Grapes........9¢
Bagel.........19¢
Muffin.........11¢

Practice **13-5**

Name________________________________

In the Bank

Number Sense

Count the coins in each bank.
Write how much money is in each bank.
Circle the bank that has the most money.

1.

_______ ¢

2.

_______ ¢

3.

_______ ¢

4.

_______ ¢

Name ______________________________

1. How much money in all?

Ⓐ 66¢

Ⓑ 69¢

Ⓒ 74¢

Ⓓ 79¢

2. Zoe sees 14 dragonflies.
Patty sees 4 dragonflies.
How many dragonflies do they see in all?

Ⓐ 20

Ⓑ 19

Ⓒ 18

Ⓓ 8

3. Draw the missing dots for 10.

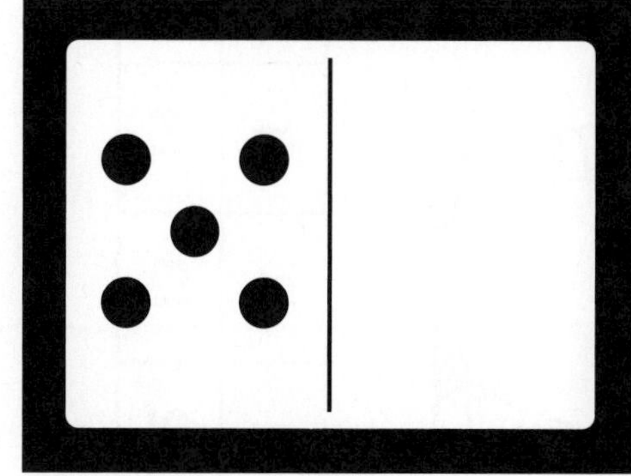

Problem of the Day 13-6

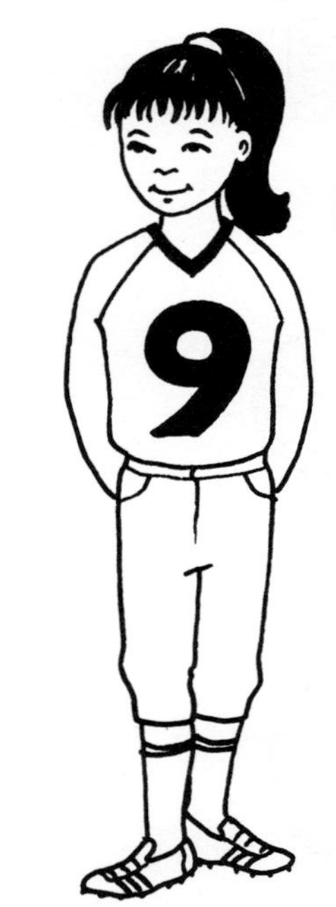

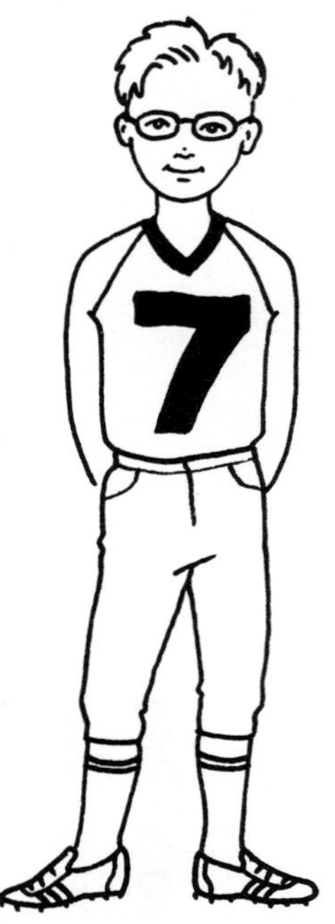

1	2	3	4	5	6	7	8	9	10
11	12	13	14	15	16	17	18	19	20

Read Aloud The team captain is a girl. She is wearing an odd number. Which child is the captain? Use this part of the hundred chart to help you find the odd number.

Name ________________________________

1. Eve bought a bucket and a shovel.
How much did Eve pay?

Ⓐ 17¢

Ⓑ 16¢

Ⓒ 15¢

Ⓓ 13¢

2. Bernice buys a pear and an apple for 12¢.
The pear costs 7¢. Which addition fact shows how much the apple costs?

Ⓐ 7¢ + 5¢ = 12¢

Ⓑ 10¢ + 2¢ = 12¢

Ⓒ 12¢ + 6¢ = 18¢

Ⓓ 12¢ + 7¢ = 19¢

3. Write prices on the tags.
Write an addition sentence to check.

Hector bought a party hat and a balloon.
Together they cost 13¢.
How much could each item cost?

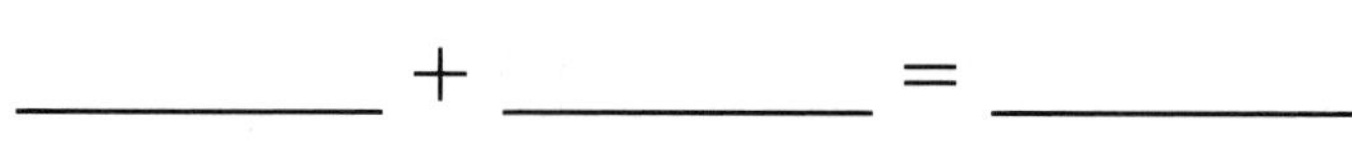

_______ + _______ = _______

Name________________________________

Problem Solving: Try, Check, and Revise

Jim bought 2 toys at the toy fair. Together they cost 11¢.
Which toys did he buy?

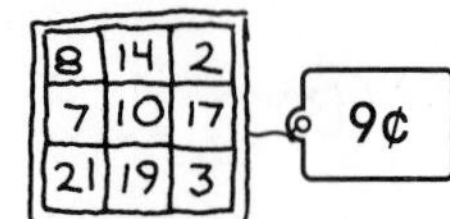

Pick 2 toys. Find their total.

Try  and .

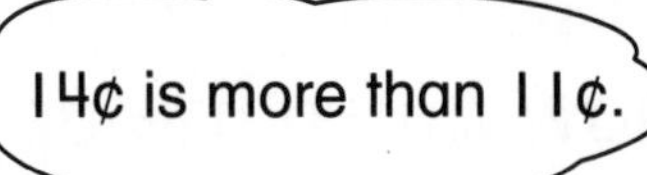

Add. ___6___¢ + ___8___¢ = ___14___¢

Find a toy that costs less than  .

The  costs less.

Try the and .

Add. ___6___¢ + ___5___¢ = ___11___¢

Jim bought the and .

1. Circle the 2 toys that cost 15¢.
Write an addition sentence to check your answer.

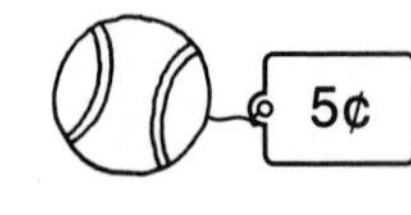

_______¢ + _______¢ = _______¢

Name______________________________

Problem Solving: Try, Check, and Revise

Circle the stickers each child bought.
Write an addition sentence to check.

  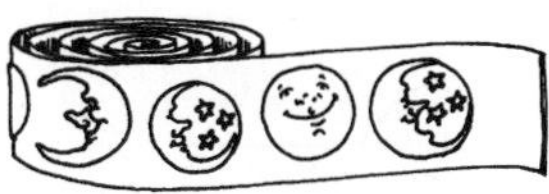 

4¢ 5¢ 8¢ 9¢

1. Venus bought 2 different stickers. Together they cost 14¢. What did Venus buy?

 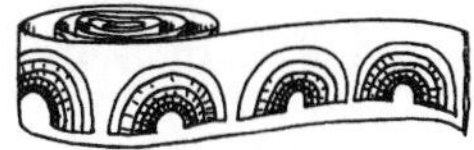

__5__¢ + ________¢ = ________¢

2. Kevin bought 2 different stickers. Together they cost 17¢. What did Kevin buy?

 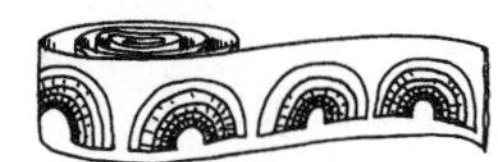

________¢ + ________¢ = ________¢

Number Sense

3. Carlos bought 2 different stickers. Together they cost 9¢. What did Carlos buy?

  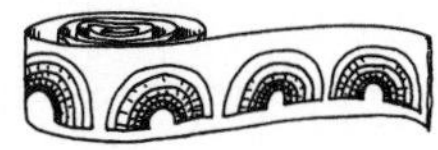

Name____

Enrichment
13-6

At the Museum Store

Read each problem. Solve. **Algebra**

Then write an addition sentence to check your work.

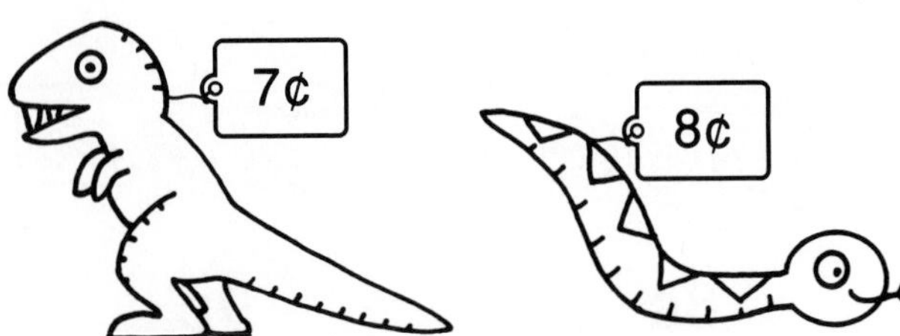

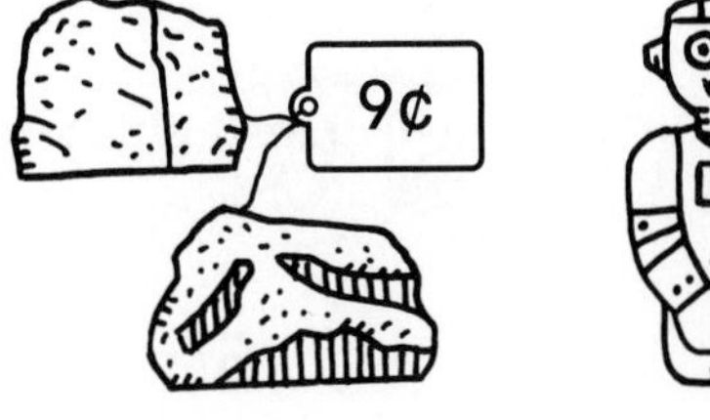

1. Lyn spends 16¢.
She buys the rocks.
Circle the other toy she buys.

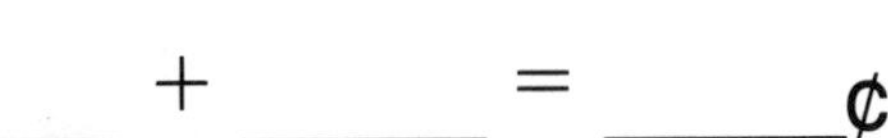

2. Paul spends 18¢.
He buys the robot.
Circle the other toy he buys.

_____ + _____ = _____¢

3. Sara spends 15¢.
She buys 2 things.
One is the snake.
Circle the other toy she buys.

4. Eric spends 17¢.
He buys the dinosaur.
Circle another toy he buys.

_____ + _____ = _____¢

Enrichment **13-6**

Name____

Mark the best answer.

1. Tory uses all these coins to buy a pencil. How much does the pencil cost?

Ⓐ 7¢

Ⓑ 20¢

Ⓒ 23¢

Ⓓ 70¢

2. Dre has 25¢. He has 12 coins. 10 of the coins are pennies. Which are Dre's other coins?

Ⓓ  

3. How much money is there in all?

Ⓐ \$1.50

Ⓑ \$1.00

Ⓒ 75¢

Ⓓ 50¢

4. Madhuri wants to buy glitter for 79¢. She has these coins. Which other coin does she need?

Name________________________________

Mark the best answer.

5. How much money is there in all?

Ⓐ 55¢

Ⓑ 45¢

Ⓒ 30¢

Ⓓ 10¢

---

6. Rosemary spent exactly 66¢. Which addition sentence shows the items that Rosemary bought?

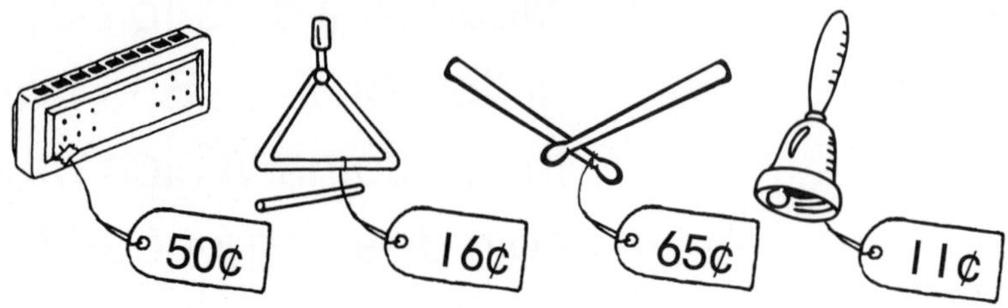

Ⓐ 65¢ + 16¢ = 81¢

Ⓑ 11¢ + 65¢ = 76¢

Ⓒ 16¢ + 50¢ = 66¢

Ⓓ 16¢ + 11¢ = 27¢

Name______________________________

Mark the best answer.

1. Count the nickels by 5s.

5¢ 10¢ _____ ¢

_____ ¢ _____ ¢

2. Circle the coins that Jeannine can use to buy the doll.

3. Nicholas spends 28¢. Circle the shells he buys.

4. Autumn has 25¢. Label Autumn's coins.

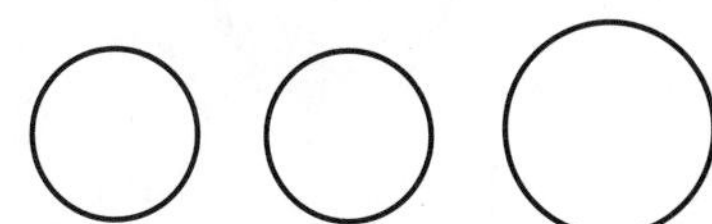

Name________________________________

5. Charlie has 50¢ in all.
Label the missing coin.

6. Skip count. Then write how much money in all.

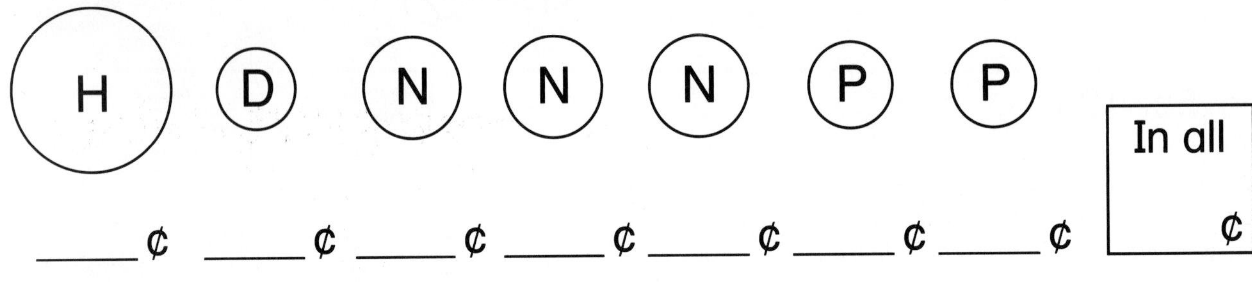

7. Both banks have the same amount of money.
Label the coins in the bank on the right.

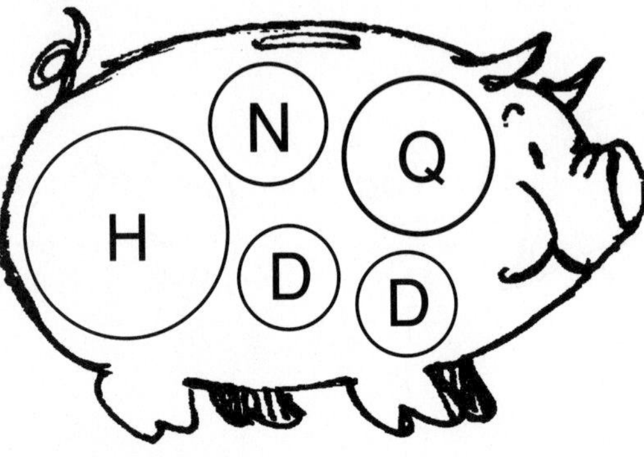

8. **Writing in Math**
Kerry bought these art supplies.
She spent 20¢.
Write prices for the art supplies on the tags.
Write an addition sentence to check your work.

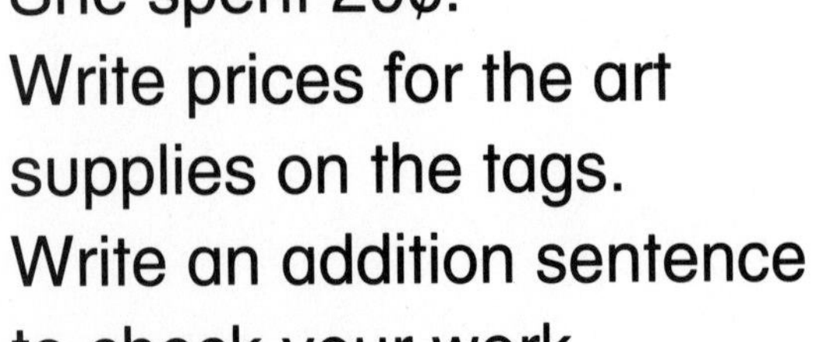

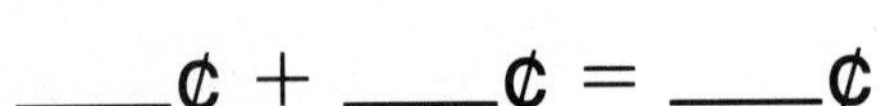

Topic 13
Free-Response Test

Name ______________________________

Bananas	Oranges	Apples	Grapes

57¢	34¢	17¢	73¢

1. Make an X on the fruit that costs the least.
Circle the coins that match the price.

D D N N P P P

---

2. Count on. Then write how much money in all.

Q D D N N P P

_____¢ _____¢ _____¢ _____¢ _____¢ _____¢ _____¢

In All
¢

Which fruit could you buy? ____________________

---

3. Write the name of a different fruit. ____________________

How much does it cost? ______ ¢

Circle the coins that match the price.

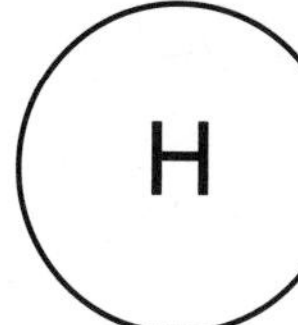        

H D D N N P P P P

Notes